ABOUT PHONICS FIRST!

Dear Reader:

This book of activities gives children practice in learning the various sounds of the alphabet, helping them decode new words as well as build on their knowledge of previously learned words. The activities cover a wide variety of topics including consonant blends and digraphs, vowels, rhyming words, homophones, silent letters, prefixes, suffixes, root words, plural, syllables, and more.

Many of the worksheets engage children in "thinking out" new words and putting them in sentence context. Others ask students to select a correct answer from several choices. Some have students working with a partner or using a dictionary to create word lists not found on the worksheet. The words are age-appropriate and the reading selections have been created using the Spache Readability Formula.

These activities can be used in any reading program with children of all ability levels. They provide the extra practice that most children need as they continue to master intermediate reading skills.

Sincerely,

Wilma H. Miller

ISBN 0-13-041461-1

CONTENTS

Worksheets

Contents

Name_____ Date_____

Follow the directions to see if you can figure out all of the secret messages.
Write each secret message on the lines below the clues.

1. Take **th** from **this** and put in **H**.

   Take **fr** from **frog** and put in **d**.

   Take **p** from **paw** and put in **s**.

   Take **c** from **come** and put in **s**.

   Take **r** from **rakes** and put in **sn**.

   Take **p** from **past** and put in **l**.

   Take **br** from **bright** and put in **n**.

   What is the secret message?

   _____

   _____

2. Take **wh** from **why** and put in **M**.

   Take **m** from **mother** and put in **br**.

   Take **sk** from **skill** and put in **w**.

   Take **fr** from **fry** and put in **tr**.

   Take **d** from **do** and put in **t**.

   Take **cl** from **clear** and put in **sp**.

   Take **c** from **come** and put in **s**.

   Take **w** from **wish** and put in **f**.

   Take **fl** from **flat** and don't put any other letter in.

   Take **fr** from **fright** and put in **n**.

   What is the secret message?

   _____

   _____

(Turn page)

3. Take **br** from **brim** and put in **T**.

   Take **dr** from **drill** and put in **w**.

   Take **pl** from **pleat** and put in **b**.

   Take **cr** from **crack** and put in **J**.

   Take **h** from **hot** and put in **n**.

   Take **pl** from **plan** and put in **D**.

   Take **h** from **hand** and don't put any other letter in.

   Take **sl** from **slim** and put in **J**.

   Take **th** from **then** and put in **wh**.

   Take **h** from **hey** and put in **th**.

   Take **gr** from **gray** and put in **pl**.

   Take **w** from **wall** and put in **b**.

   What is the secret message?

   _____

   _____

Name_____ Date_____

Follow the directions to see if you can figure out all of the secret messages.
Write each secret message on the lines below the clues.

1. Take **fl** from **fly** and put in **M**.

   Take **m** from **mitten** and put in **k**.

   Take **m** from **mill** and put in **w**.

   Take **th** from **thump** and put in **j**.

   Take **th** from **then** and put in **wh**.

   Take **w** from **we** and put in **sh**.

   Take **pl** from **plan** and put in **c**.

   Take **kn** from **knee** and put in **s**.

   Take **spr** from **spring** and put in **str**.

   ### What is the secret message?

   _____

   _____

2. Take **h** from **his** and put in **Th**.

   Take **sl** from **slack** and put in **bl**.

   Take **br** from **brake** and put in **sn**.

   Take **sk** from **skill** and put in **w**.

   Take **m** from **mill** and put in **k**.

   Take **n** from **nice** and put in **m**.

   Take **h** from **hen** and put in **wh**.

   Take **spl** from **split** and don't put any other letter in.

   Take **cl** from **clan** and put in **c**.

   ### What is the secret message?

   _____

   _____

(Turn page)

3. Take **w** from **we** and add **Sh**.

   Take **t** from **tiles** and add **sm**.

   Take **m** from **men** and add **wh**.

   Take **tr** from **try** and add **m**.

   Take **fr** from **frog** and add **d**.

   Take **cl** from **clumps** and add **j**.

What is the secret message?

_____

_____

Name_____ Date_____

Read each sentence silently. Look at the initial consonant at the beginning of the blank space in each sentence. In each blank space write a <u>complete</u> word that begins with the correct initial consonant <u>and</u> also makes sense in the sentence. You may use your dictionary for the correct spelling of any word you don't know how to spell. You may work with a partner(s) if you want.

1. It can be great fun to paddle a **c**_____ down a river.

2. The judge gave the burglar a **s**_____ of five years in prison.

3. The **p**_____ in Antarctica look like small men wearing black-and-white evening clothes.

4. It is very exciting to **d**_____ a Christmas tree with gaily colored strings of lights and ornaments.

5. Juana watched the **m**_____ pull a rabbit out of a hat.

6. My Halloween **c**_____ is going to be a black-and-white skeleton.

7. The **p**_____ who went West in covered wagons usually were very courageous.

8. In school most children enjoy **r**_____ so that they can go outside and play on the playground.

9. Before electric lights were invented, people sometimes used **c**_____ for light.

(Turn page)

10. The **k**_____ is an animal that lives in Australia and jumps long distances on its very strong hind legs.

11. Mr. Ching is a very optimistic and **h**_____ man.

12. When Mary Anne was sleeping last night, she had a very frightening **n**_____.

13. A **v**_____ is a musical instrument with four strings that is played with a bow.

14. Wisconsin is so cold in the winter that it sometimes gets below **z**_____.

15. When she put on her **p**_____, Mrs. Shepherd smelled very nice.

Name_____ Date_____

Read each sentence silently. Select the one word below each sentence that contains the same consonant blend as the key word <u>and</u> makes sense in the sentence. Write the correct word in the blank space. Reread the sentence to be sure it is correct.

1. <u>principal</u>

   The state of Nebraska contains some _____ land.

   range   prairie   prickle

2. <u>grind</u>

   Mrs. Angelo was very _____ to the paramedics who

   saved her life when she had a heart attack.

   thankful   ground   grateful

3. <u>drench</u>

   After watching the late movie on television, my father felt

   _____.

   drowsy   sleepy   draft

4. <u>pleasure</u>

   Stars and _____ are both part of our universe.

   planets   moons   plural

5. <u>specimen</u>

   My grandmother felt _____ when we celebrated her

   eightieth birthday.

   glasses   spirit   special

(Turn page)

6. <u>drink</u>

I _____ having to take that science test because
I haven't studied for it.

       dislike   dread   dragon

7. <u>plod</u>

One very beautiful and valuable metal is _____.

       platinum   plaid   silver

8. <u>stern</u>

Mr. Gettys may need to get a _____ or two on his
forehead after bumping it on the beam.

       stood   scratch   stitch

9. <u>brow</u>

Maria _____ for a long time after her puppy
disappeared.

       brooded   worried   breathe

10. <u>scream</u>

Elian _____ his knee very badly when he fell over
a large boulder.

       scraped   injured   script

Name_____ Date_____

Write in each blank the word that begins with the same consonant blend as the underlined word. The word you write in the blank also should make sense in the sentence.

1. When my mother shook the pillow, the _____ feathers <u>fluttered</u> to the floor.

        soft   fluffy   flour

2. I caught a <u>glimpse</u> of a _____ high up in the sky.

        glider   gloomy   airplane

3. The _____ farmer was trying to sell his <u>stock</u> because he needed the money very badly.

        serious   stride   stern

4. The _____ man <u>scolded</u> me for not believing as he did.

        scornful   contemptuous   score

5. The right to vote is a <u>precious</u> _____.

        prairie   privilege   right

6. That fierce _____ <u>blew</u> in from the west.

        blizzard   snowstorm   blackened

(Turn page)

7. The _____ engineer designed a long <u>bridge</u> over the river.

        clever   brilliant   bruise

8. The <u>twins</u> are going snowmobiling just after _____.

        twilight   sunset   twitch

9. I will have to _____ fertilizer on my garden this <u>spring</u>.

        scatter   spread   sprawl

10. Mr. Wong was <u>spellbound</u> by the _____ sight he saw.

        spectacular   unusual   spare

11. It takes great <u>skill</u> to _____ through reading material.

        skim   look   sky

12. Mrs. Tucci _____will have a <u>problem</u> making Carlo behave.

        likely   program   probably

13. The man <u>slouched</u> in his chair because he was _____ after being up all night fighting the fire.

        sleepy   tired   slander

Name_____   **Date**_____

Read each word below. Notice that the words reflect the <u>soft</u> and <u>hard</u> sounds of <u>c</u> and the soft sound of g. After you have read each word, write its correct spelling on the line beside it. You may use a dictionary if you want. You may also work with a partner(s) if you would like. The first one is done for you.

1. jypsy   _____gypsy_____

2. kanary   _____

3. resite   _____

4. sity   _____

5. sentury   _____

6. jym   _____

7. bisykle   _____

8. syklone   _____

9. seiling   _____

10. jentle   _____

11. senter   _____

12. sellar   _____

13. jeneral   _____

14. kause   _____

(Turn page)

15. raje

_____

16. chanje

_____

17. jem

_____

18. jinjer

_____

19. aje

_____

20. nise

_____

Name_____ **Date**_____

Read each word below. Notice that the words reflect the <u>soft</u> and <u>hard</u> sounds of <u>c</u> and the soft sound of <u>g</u>. After you have read each word, write its correct spelling on the line beside it. You may use a dictionary if you want. You may also work with a partner(s) if you would like. The first one is done for you.

1. enjine   _____ engine _____

2. twise   _____

3. sitizen   _____

4. sement   _____

5. voise   _____

6. komik   _____

7. kane   _____

8. sirkle   _____

9. komb   _____

10. sensus   _____

11. sypress   _____

12. koat   _____

13. jiant   _____

14. kurly   _____

(Turn page)

15. kapsule   _____

16. pensil   _____

17. deside   _____

18. danjer   _____

19. enerjy   _____

20. persent   _____

Name_____ **Date**_____

Read each sentence silently. There are four words under each sentence. In the blank space write the word that makes sense in the sentence.

1. A _____ is a large mass of ice and snow that moves very slowly down a mountain or across land until it melts.

   glorious   glacier   glacial   gladiator

2. The man certainly made a _____ when he sold his property at a very low cost to the land developer.

   bleach   blemish   blunder   blossom

3. The art of making pictures with a camera is called _____.

   photography   philosophy   physicist   physical

4. The sculptor had to use a _____ to shape the block of stone for the statue.

   chocolate   chipmunk   chisel   charcoal

5. Medicine and law are considered to be two _____.

   processions   progress   professions   pressure

6. The linguist _____ the speech of the Chinese leader into English.

   transported   translated   triumphant   tremendous

(Turn page)

7. The _____ on our house need to be painted this year.

   shimmer   shutters   shillings   shrimp

8. A rock formed from clay or mud is called _____.

   shambles   shadow   shale   shampoo

9. Mr. Goldman is going to attempt to clear the _____ on his property next Saturday.

   thicket   theory   theft   thimble

10. A _____ is a platform built out over the water so that ships can load and unload.

    whisk   whittle   wharf   wheeze

Name_____ **Date**_____

Read each sentence silently. Then select the one word below the sentence that contains the same <u>consonant digraph</u> as the key word <u>and</u> makes sense in the sentence. Write this word in the blank space and reread the sentence to make sure it is correct.

1. <u>whimper</u>

   Patti and Rosa built a wooden clubhouse and then decided they would have

   to put _____ shutters on it.

          paint   white   whirlwind

2. <u>shadow</u>

   The British use _____ as part of their monetary system.

          shillings   pounds   shimmer

3. <u>theory</u>

   When Dustin tried to perform a dangerous trick on his skateboard, he fell off

   and injured his _____.

          shoulder   thigh   thicket

4. <u>photography</u>

   Our grandfather tells us spooky stories at Halloween about imaginary

   _____.

          phonograph   ghosts   phantoms

5. <u>phase</u>

   The most difficult part of reading for Ellie always has been

   _____.

          phonics   phobia   comprehension

(Turn page)

6. <u>whippoorwill</u>

The _____ is a very interesting breed of dog that often

can be seen at a dog show.

        greyhound   whippet   whistle

7. <u>thatched</u>

The _____ is an extremely useful weather instrument.

        thermometer   barometer   thistle

8. <u>photograph</u>

Mr. Thomas made an important error in the last _____

of the science experiment.

        step   phase   phony

9. <u>then</u>

Many people _____ San Francisco is the most

beautiful city in the United States.

        which   think   though

10. <u>rough</u>

This porterhouse steak certainly tastes _____ and

leathery.

        touch   tough   though

Name_____ Date_____

> Read each sentence silently. Then select the one word underneath the sentence that contains the same <u>rime</u> or <u>suffix</u> as the key word <u>and</u> makes sense in the sentence. Write this word in the blank space and reread the sentence to make sure it is correct.

1. <u>inscription</u>

   There was intense _____ between Joey and Jeff

   to determine who could hurl the javelin farther in the track-and-field meet.

         rivalry   competition   recreation

2. <u>vicious</u>

   The fox is perhaps one of the most _____

   creatures that inhabits the North American continent.

         clever   ingenious   conscious

3. <u>venomous</u>

   It was truly _____ for the son of the millionaire

   to squander so much money.

         thoughtless   miraculous   preposterous

4. <u>transfusion</u>

   Many people in our country feel a strong _____ for

   eating the meat of a reptile although it tastes very much like chicken.

         revulsion   succession   dislike

(Turn page)

5. <u>incongruous</u>

It was very _____ of Ms. Marks to resign from her

well-paid position as an executive before obtaining another suitable position

in the software business.

impulsive   impetuous   innocuous

6. <u>flight</u>

Although the new principal was a _____ man, he was

very forceful and firm when it became necessary.

slender   slight   floodlight

7. <u>rapidly</u>

Spring came _____ this year, and many of the buds

on the deciduous trees froze when it became colder again.

prematurely   lastly   nature

8. <u>high</u>

The elderly woman had to _____ when she realized

she had been swindled out of her life savings.

grieve   sigh   plight

9. <u>brick</u>

The _____ over the oil well in Oklahoma was

demolished during a severe explosion and fire.

framework   derrick   slick

10. <u>negative</u>

I am _____ it will be beneficial for us to have a

vacation next month.

certain   narrative   positive

Name_____ **Date**_____

Read each sentence silently. Then select the one word underneath the sentence that contains the same <u>rime</u> or <u>suffix</u> as the key word <u>and</u> makes sense in the sentence. Write this word in the blank space and reread the sentence to make sure it is correct.

1. <u>persuasive</u>

   Glue is very _____.

           cohesive   sticky   decisive

2. <u>convention</u>

   The _____ in our government during the Watergate period was extremely shocking.

           corruption   depravity   prescription

3. <u>porous</u>

   That _____ sky may well foretell an impending tornado.

           threatening   populous   ominous

4. <u>recession</u>

   Our class is planning to make an interesting _____ to Washington, D.C. in early spring.

           excursion   trip   submission

5. <u>wisdom</u>

   Many countries fought for their _____ during the two world wars.

           freedom   nationhood   religion

(Turn page)

6. government

   In her opening _____ she tried to explain her position on tax cuts.

         development   speech   statement

7. upward

   Kim took a step _____ in order to reach the high beam.

         forward   foreword   eastward

8. jewelry

   Native Americans who live in the southwest make beautiful _____ out of clay and other natural ingredients.

         cutlery   pottery   statues

9. competent

   We discovered that barium was a _____ element from sodium.

         excellent   accident   different

10. goodness

   When _____ fell, primitive man became concerned for the safety of his family.

         darkness   kindness   evening

11. fright

   Early suffragettes worked hard for the _____ of women to vote.

         equality   right   freedom

Name_____ Date_____

Read the words in the box. Then read each question below. Select the correct answer from the words in the box and write it on the line next to the question. (A word may be used only once. Not all of the words will be used.)

bamboo	meek	few	rough	bounce
seal	fright	smear	shoot	stick
precious	pattern	whirlpool	twenty	hook
glider	chimpanzee	spectacular	those	skirt
shield	volcano	high	draft	troop

1. What word rhymes with <u>sigh</u>? ____ _____

2. What word contains the same diphthong as <u>fountain</u>?

   _____

3. What word rhymes with <u>tough</u>? _____

4. What word begins with the same consonant digraph as <u>whisper</u>?

   _____

5. What word begins with the same consonant as <u>banner</u>?

   _____

6. What word rhymes with <u>hurt</u>? _____

7. What word begins with the same consonant digraph as <u>charcoal</u>?

   _____

(Turn page)

8. What word begins with the same consonant blend as <u>dreadful</u>?

_____

9. What word begins with the same consonant blend as <u>sparkle</u>?

_____

10. What word begins with the same consonant digraph as <u>themselves</u>?

_____

11. What word contains the same double <u>o</u> sound as <u>stood</u>?

_____

12. What word begins with the same consonant as <u>vocabulary</u>?

_____

13. What word rhymes with <u>light</u>? _____

14. What word begins with the same consonant blend as <u>twitch</u>?

_____

15. What word begins with the same consonant blend as <u>prairie</u>?

_____

Name_____ **Date**_____

➡ Write the plurals for each of these words, either <u>s</u> or <u>es</u>. The first is done for you.

1. chair   _____chairs_____   13. cross   _____

2. boss   _____   14. college_____

3. gulf   _____   15. trench   _____

4. video   _____   16. fox   _____

5. dish   _____   17. fish   _____

6. bench   _____   18. match   _____

7. belief   _____   19. tax   _____

8. radio   _____   20. brush   _____

9. booklet   _____   21. pencil   _____

10. toss   _____   22. lunch   _____

11. cliff   _____   23. wish   _____

12. wax   _____   24. studio   _____

Name_____ **Date**_____

Write plurals for each of these words. For some of the words you change y to i and add <u>es</u>. For the other words you add only an <u>s</u>. The first word is done for you.

1. city _____cities_____   11. baby _____

2. valley _____   12. turkey _____

3. key _____   13. caddy _____

4. family _____   14. variety _____

5. candy _____   15. spy _____

6. play _____   16. employ _____

7. army _____   17. lady _____

8. puppy _____   18. fly _____

9. boy _____   19. cherry _____

10. trolley _____   20. joy _____

You may use a dictionary or work with a partner to find the plurals of four different words that end in y. Make sure two of the plurals end in <u>ies</u> and the other two end in <u>s</u>.

y to <u>ies</u>:   1. _____   _____

2. _____   _____

y plus <u>s</u>:   1. _____   _____

2. _____   _____

15

Name_____ Date_____

On many words that end with f or fe, you need to change f to v and add es. There are some words that end in f where you need to add only an s. Write the plurals for the words. The first two are done for you.

1. gulf _____gulfs_____   9. chief _____

2. leaf _____leaves_____   10. wife _____

3. cliff _____   11. roof _____

4. knife _____   12. life _____

5. thief _____   13. wolf _____

6. belief _____   14. dwarf _____

7. half _____   15. scarf _____

8. loaf _____   16. puff _____

You may use a dictionary or work with a partner to find the plurals of five different words that end with f or fe:

1. _____   _____

2. _____   _____

3. _____   _____

4. _____   _____

5. _____   _____

16

Name_____ Date_____

Write a suffix after the root word to match the definition shown to the right.
The first is done for you.

1. sight _____less_____   without sight, blind

2. joy _____   full of joy

3. penman _____   skill or art of writing

4. week _____   every week

5. child _____   like a child

6. nervous _____   state of being nervous

7. thought _____   doing without thought

8. fail _____   the act of failing

9. warm _____   in a warm way

10. teach _____   one who teaches

11. worth _____   without worth

12. loyal _____   the state of being loyal

13. length _____   to make long

14. state _____   the act of saying something

15. popular _____   to make popular

17

Name_____ Date_____

Write a prefix before the root word to match the definition shown to the right.
The first is done for you.

1. __dys__ function   does not function well

2. _____ justice   not just

3. _____ regular   not usual or regular

4. _____ ground   below ground

5. _____ active   too much activity

6. _____ board   going on a ship

7. _____ spell   to spell incorrectly

8. _____ continue   to stop

9. _____ possible   not possible

10. _____ marine   under water

11. _____ circle   half of a circle

12. _____ cycle   to use again

13. _____ certain   not sure

14. _____ night   in the middle of the night

15. _____ legal   not legal

18

Name_____ **Date**_____

Some words have a prefix or a suffix. A few words have both a prefix and a suffix. Underline the prefixes and circle the suffixes. Then write the root words on the blank lines. The first is done for you.

1. <u>un</u>comfort(able)　　　　　comfort _____

2. withhold　　　　　_____

3. progressive　　　　　_____

4. bicycle　　　　　_____

5. economical　　　　　_____

6. backward　　　　　_____

7. marketwise　　　　　_____

8. underground　　　　　_____

9. postscript　　　　　_____

10. discontinue　　　　　_____

11. childish　　　　　_____

12. unemotional　　　　　_____

13. equidistant　　　　　_____

14. honesty　　　　　_____

(Turn page)

15. schoolwise _____

16. friendship _____

17. discontinue _____

18. unfortunate _____

19. antisocial _____

20. misbehave _____

21. honorary _____

22. thoughtful _____

23. government _____

24. ultramodern _____

25. hyperactive _____

26. afternoon _____

27. standardization _____

28. publisher _____

29. assistant _____

30. encouragement _____

Name_____ Date_____

 Here are twenty words that begin with consonants. One of the consonants is silent. As you read each word, put a line (/) across the silent consonant. The first one is done for you.

1. K̸nit
11. g n a r l

2. g n a t
12. k n o c k

3. w r o n g
13. g n a s h

4. w r i s t
14. w r i t t e n

5. k n i g h t
15. k n e e c a p

6. g n a w
16. w r i n g

7. k n a p s a c k
17. k n e e l

8. w r e s t l e
18. k n u c k l e

9. g n u
19. g n o m e

10. k n o t
20. k n o w l e d g e

 Can you think of three other words with a silent consonant in them? You may use a dictionary or work with a partner if you want.

_____ _____ _____

Name_____ **Date**_____

Put in the silent letters that were left out of the following words. Write the correct word on the blank line. The first one is done for you.

1. gost _____ghost_____

2. nob _____

3. rong _____

4. nife _____

5. nat _____

6. rinkle _____

7. neel _____

8. nome _____

9. nuckle _____

10. rite _____

11. rench _____

12. narl _____

13. gastly _____

14. nack _____

15. wip _____

16. restle _____

17. getto _____

18. reath _____

19. neecap _____

20. nife _____

Can you think of any other words with silent letters in them? Write at least four of them on the following lines:

_____   _____

_____   _____

21

Name_____ **Date**_____

⇨ Say the following words to yourself. If there are any silent letters in them, put a line through them. The first one is done for you.

1. c r i m ~~e~~

2. s a c k

3. f o u r

4. b l o w

5. h a v e

6. g u e s s

7. w r e n

8. d o u b t

9. t h r o w

10. k n i t

11. s t i t c h

12. p l u m b

13. k h a k i

14. s i g h

15. t h e r e

16. g u a r d

17. c u d d l e

18. l a m b

19. g h a s t l y

20. w r o n g

21. b r i g h t

22. b e f o r e

23. s e n s e

24. b e e n

25. t h o u g h

26. s n o r e

27. t w o

28. u n w r a p

29. s u b t l e

30. l e a r n

31. c r u m b

32. d a u g h t e r

33. r a c e t r a c k

34. o f t e n

35. g u i d e

36. p i t c h

⇨ Can you think of three other words that have a silent vowel or a silent consonant in them?

_____ _____ _____

Name_____ Date_____

Read this story about a class that had a special treat one Saturday afternoon. <u>Most</u> of the silent letters have been left out of the words in the story. As you read the story, cross out each word whose <u>silent letters</u> have been omitted and write the correct spelling of the word above it. When you have finished, reread the story to be sure you have found all of the words with omitted silent letters.

A Special Treat

(1)   Mrs. Ellison's fifth-grad clas had been extremly busy for several

(2)   weks. In fact, it semed to them that they had worked da and nit. Al of the

(3)   students in her clas had been colecting mone for ech person in the neborhood

(4)   to help the children who hav muscular dystrophy, a dises that cripls

(5)   children and often confins them to a whelchair. After the students in her

(6)   clas had colected ninty-four dolars, Mrs. Ellison thout it was tim to

(7)   reward them with a special tret for al their eforts.

(8)   She sugested that the clas hav a roler skating party at a rink

(9)   several mils from the school on the next Satrday afternoon. Many of the

(10)   children had never skated at a rink, and they rely didn't no what to expect.

(11)   They wer extremly excited about it anywa. Of cours, a few of the students

(12)   in the clas had skated ner their homs at som tim or other. Several of the

(13)   students couldn't roler skat at al, but they were anxious to try.

(Turn page)

(14)   Al of the children in the clas met at the rink rit at two o'clock on

(15)   Saturday afternoon. Ech child was given a pair of roler skats that wer the

(16)   rit siz. When the children put on ther skats, several of them fel down but

(17)   quickly got up and trid agan. Altho som of the children skated very wel

(18)   alon or with a partner, it was a very funy sit to se others try to skat.

(19)   Several children trid grabing onto som metal bars that were ner the wals of

(20)   the rink. Other children simply fel down and got up agan usualy laughing

(21)   at themselves. However, most of the children skated fairly wel by the end

(22)   of the afternn.

(23)   Befor they went hom, ech of them had hamburgers and Coks.

(24)   Somhow the hamburgers at the rink seemed to tast better than the

(25)   hamburgers they had eten at hom. When it was tim to go hom, al of the

(26)   children in Mrs. Ellison's clas agred that Saturday had ben a rely special

(27)   da, and they hopd that they mit be abl to go roler skating at the rink agn

(28)   somda.

Name_____ **Date**_____

When two vowels are together, the first one often has a long sound and the second one is silent. In the following words, circle the long vowel and put a line through the short vowel. The first one is done for you.

1. m @ i̸ d

2. s t e a l

3. g l u e

4. p e a c h

5. c l a i m

6. t r i e d

7. f r u i t

8. c h e a p

9. p r e a c h

10. c o a c h

11. c o a s t

12. p r a i s e

13. s t r e a k

14. p a i n t

15. c l e a n

16. f u e l

17. a p p r o a c h

18. e x p l a i n

19. p e a n u t

20. c r u e l

Can you think of four other words where the first vowel is long and the second silent?

_____   _____

_____   _____

24

Name_____ Date_____

Circle the contractions found in each sentence. Then write the words that make up each contraction on the blank line. The first one is done for you.

1. Tom (doesn't) think that she will come. ____does____ ____not____

2. Koala bears aren't bears but marsupials. _____ _____

3. I'll tell you how to find the best melon in the supermarket.

   _____ _____

4. Do you think they'll be on time for the football game?

   _____ _____

5. Craig couldn't have scored 20 points for the team without their help.

   _____ _____

6. Didn't Lee mention that you have to go to the office today?

   _____ _____

7. Someday I'm going to be able to ride the subway train on my

   own. _____ _____

8. Wasn't that a sad ending for a funny movie?

   _____ _____

(Turn page)

9. Tova isn't the type of person to spread a rumor.

   _____ _____

10. They weren't paying attention to the instructions from the loudspeaker.

    _____ _____

11. If you're sure that you want to play soccer, then sign up today.

    _____ _____

12. I'd buy two more computer games if she'd lend me the money.

    _____ _____, _____ _____

13. It's raining outside, so you'd better come inside.

    _____ _____, _____ _____

14. He doesn't think that she'll come on the field trip to the museum.

    _____ _____, _____ _____

25

Name_____ Date_____

▷ Write the contractions for the words shown below. The first one is done for you.

1. I am _____I'm_____   6. they are _____

2. she is _____   7. did not _____

3. we are _____   8. will not _____

4. he is _____   9. I have _____

5. it is _____   10. there is _____

▷ Now, write the two words that form these contractions.

1. couldn't _____   6. aren't _____

2. can't _____   7. she'll _____

3. I'll _____   8. hadn't _____

4. don't _____   9. wouldn't _____

5. here's _____   10. they'll _____

26

Name_____ **Date**_____

In words with double consonants, the syllable break comes between the two consonants. On the blank lines, write the words divided into syllables. The first one is done for you.

1. batter   _____bat ter_____

2. written   _____

3. flatter   _____

4. Molly   _____

5. riddle   _____

6. appear   _____

7. happen   _____

8. filler   _____

9. trolley   _____

10. saddle   _____

11. error   _____

12. middle   _____

13. oppose   _____

14. immense   _____

15. little   _____

16. inning   _____

17. announce   _____

18. effort   _____

19. planning   _____

20. misspell   _____

See how many double consonant words you can list on the following lines:

_____   _____

_____   _____

_____   _____

27

Name_____ **Date**_____

Draw a line (/) in the following words to show where they should be divided. On the blank lines write the number of syllables for the words. The first one is done for you. **Note:** Some words have only one syllable.

1. j u n/g l e   _____2_____

2. m y s e l f   _____

3. u n d e r   _____

4. t o d a y   _____

5. c a r d   _____

6. w i t h o u t   _____

7. e x p l a i n   _____

8. s t r o n g   _____

9. f i g u r e   _____

10. l a n g u a g e   _____

11. d i s t a n c e   _____

12. r e g i o n   _____

13. m o u n t a i n   _____

14. i n f o r m a l   _____

15. s u b m a r i n e   _____

(Turn page)

16. misfortune   _____

17. undoing   _____

18. informant   _____

19. irresponsive   _____

20. distressful   _____

21. strength   _____

22. wealth   _____

28

Name_____'_____ Date_____

Draw a line (/) in the following words to show where they should be divided. On the blank line write the number of syllables found in each word. The first one is done for you.

1. e x/e r/c i s e ___3___   13. r e m e m b e r _____

2. c o m m o n _____   14. s y l l a b l e s _____

3. p a t t e r n _____   15. i n c r e d i b l e _____

4. d i f f e r e n t _____   16. d i s c o v e r _____

5. i n t e r e s t _____   17. s u d d e n l y _____

6. c e r t a i n _____   18. m a t e r n a l _____

7. t a b l e _____   19. q u i c k l y _____

8. o m i t _____   20. u n l i k e l y _____

9. r e c o r d _____   21. d e s c r i b e _____

10. v i l l a g e _____   22. s i t u a t i o n _____

11. i s l a n d _____   23. r e p r e s e n t _____

12. c a p a b l e _____   24. h o w e v e r _____

(Turn page)

SYLLABLE CHALLENGE

Write a one-syllable word: _____

Write a two-syllable word: _____

Write a three-syllable word: _____

Write a four-syllable word: _____

29

Name_____ Date_____

Words that have the vowels <u>ee</u> and <u>ea</u> usually have <u>long ē</u> sounds. Sometimes <u>ea</u> has a <u>short ĕ</u> sound. On the blank lines next to the words, write **l** for long e sounds and **s** for short e sounds. The first one is done for you.

1. eat	l	11. beef	____	21. dread	____
2. sleep	____	12. steady	____	22. peach	____
3. weapon	____	13. fifteen	____	23. green	____
4. three	____	14. meadow	____	24. heaven	____
5. ready	____	15. agree	____	25. degree	____
6. easy	____	16. head	____	26. pleasure	____
7. beat	____	17. greed	____	27. referee	____
8. eel	____	18. screen	____	28. sixteen	____
9. clean	____	19. thread	____	29. weather	____
10. weak	____	20. measure	____	30. peanut	____

Can you think of more <u>ee</u> and <u>ea</u> words? Write them on the following lines and write **l** or **s** after each for long or short e sounds:

_____ ____   _____ ____

_____ ____   _____ ____

_____ ____   _____ ____

30

Name_____ **Date**_____

Sometimes the letter y has a short ĭ sound in words (gym, oxygen). Most of the time, it has a long ē, long ī, or regular y consonant sound. After the following words, write ē, ī, or y to show the sound y makes.

1. early _____

2. shy _____

3. yellow _____

4. country _____

5. cycle _____

6. beyond _____

7. deny _____

8. youth _____

9. heavy _____

10. barnyard _____

11. many _____

12. energy _____

13. python _____

14. quickly _____

15. lawyer _____

16. rhyme _____

17. usually _____

18. geography _____

19. reply _____

20. style _____

21. hyphen _____

22. your _____

23. myself _____

24. everything _____

31

Name_____ Date_____

Synonyms are words that have similar meanings. Match the words in the first column that are most similar to the words in the second column. One is done for you.

1. keep   rush   2. junk   often

   story   finish   strength   annoy

   income   hold   frequent   shut

   end   tale   bother   power

   hurry   earnings   close   waste

3. work   silent   4. vast   worth

   still   blunder   try   fresh

   take   ache   find   attempt

   mistake   labor   value   huge

   pain   grab   new   locate

32

Name_____ Date_____

Antonyms are words that mean the opposite of each other. Match the words in the first column that are the opposite of the words in the second column. One is done for you.

1. above   straight

    easy   fact

    crooked   below

    fiction   full

    empty   hard

2. tall   south

    teacher   slow

    north   laugh

    rapid   student

    weep   short

3. wet   then

    top   dry

    now   forget

    sour   sweet

    remember   bottom

4. hurry   friend

    often   freeze

    melt   tame

    stranger   slow

    wild   seldom

33

Name_____ Date_____

Write the antonym or synonym of each of the following words. Make sure that the words have the same endings. The first one is done for you.

1. adds   (synonym)   _____totals_____

2. higher   (synonym)   _____

3. finished   (antonym)   _____

4. happiness   (antonym)   _____

5. walked   (synonym)   _____

6. pages   (synonym)   _____

7. loving   (antonym)   _____

8. allows   (antonym)   _____

9. hurrying   (synonym)   _____

10. guessing   (antonym)   _____

11. gladly   (synonym)   _____

12. wrecked   (antonym)   _____

13. hurried   (antonym)   _____

14. dangerous   (synonym)   _____

15. robbers   (synonym)   _____

(Turn page)

Create four antonyms and synonyms on your own:

Antonyms: 1. _____ _____

2. _____ _____

3. _____ _____

4. _____ _____

Synonyms: 1. _____ _____

2. _____ _____

3. _____ _____

4. _____ _____

Name_____ **Date**_____

➡ Circle the compound words found in the following sentences. The first one is done for you.

1. His (birthday) was January 1, 2000.

2. Kim's grandmother served us oatmeal for breakfast.

3. The outlaw stole the mailman's truck.

4. Somewhere to the left of the table is the hairbrush.

5. Can she put the popcorn in her raincoat?

6. We went onto the railroad car as soon as the policeman said it was safe.

7. The rainbow appeared in the southwest part of the sky after the sunshine returned.

8. There was a blueberry stain on Rosemarie's new raincoat.

9. Our whole class decided to eat peanuts and cupcakes for a snack on our class trip.

10. The shipmate survived the shipwreck sometime in the evening by jumping into a lifeboat.

11. We need to highlight all the words in the newspaper article that tell what things are sold in drugstores.

(Turn page)

12. The dragonfly flew over the doghouse and then landed on the football outside of it.

13. Our family went on a steamboat ride over the weekend to listen to the storyteller's tales about the Mississippi River.

14. Lela was homesick for her family when she went inside the empty bedroom.

15. Chuck's birthday party gave everyone an earache from the loud noise.

35

Name_____ Date_____

Sometimes words sound the same but have different meanings. These words are called <u>homophones</u>. Underline the homophone that makes the most sense for the following sentences. The first one is done for you.

1. Jackie (eight, <u>ate</u>) his dinner at the (<u>steak</u>, stake) restaurant last night.

2. Will you (write, right, rite) him about (who's, whose) going to the soccer match?

3. (Some, Sum) animals take care of their young for years, but most animals (do, due, dew) take care of their young for at least a year.

4. She plans to (sell, cell) her mother's (knew, new) lamp at the fund raiser.

5. Alex took a step (forward, foreword) so he could smell the (flower, flour) better.

6. Did you (know, no) that (there, their, they're) are seven kittens in the litter?

7. Nancy looked (pale, pail) when she saw a (pair, pare) of puppies on the street.

8. We traveled to (our, hour) home in the country to see the (deer, dear) in the backyard.

9. If Craig would (steal, steel) first base, his baseball team (would, wood) win the game that (knight, night).

10. Politicians like to see the results of (polls, poles) so they know what (you, yew, ewe) are thinking.

(Turn page)

11. Grandmother (beat, beet) the eggs in the recipe for her (desert, dessert).

12. The (stairs, stares) in the office building are (higher, hire) than those in the (wood, would) mill.

13. Our school's best athlete felt (week, weak) when he saw the (bare, bear) running on the track.

14. We went to the jewelry (sale, sail) to see if we could buy some fourteen (carrot, karat) gold rings.

15. They haven't decided (whether, weather) to eat a (piece, peace) of chocolate fudge or a (bowl, boll) of ice cream.

36

Name_____ Date_____

Who's and whose sound the same, but they do not mean the same thing. Who's is a contraction for "who is" or "who has." Whose is a possessive word that shows ownership. Select the right word for each sentence.

1. _____ hat is on the dining room table?

2. I need to find out _____ going to the meeting this afternoon.

3. _____ the driver of the sports car?

4. _____ books are going to be returned to the library?

5. If that game is yours, then _____ game is this?

6. In their meeting, they needed to decide _____ going to be in charge of the treasury.

You're and your sound the same, but they do not mean the same thing either. You're is a contraction for "you are." Your is a possessive word that shows ownership. Select the right word for each sentence.

1. You must remember to lock _____ room when you leave it.

2. _____ much younger than I thought.

3. Be careful where _____ going after the dance.

(Turn page)

4. According to the flight schedule, _____ on Flight 209 to Chicago.

5. Do you know where I put _____ video game?

6. I don't know if these are _____ jacket and keys or mine.

37

Name_____ Date_____

Some words are spelled the same, but have different meanings. These are called <u>homographs</u>. Some homographs are also heteronyms. Heteronyms have different pronunciations, like close (shut) and close (near). Circle the correct meaning for each of the homographs in the following sentences. The first one is done for you.

1. Mindy had a bad <u>case</u> of measles the night before her piano recital.

    (condition)   box or container   upper part of the body

2. Jack put a <u>band</u> together to earn some extra money.

    thin strip for binding   group of musicians   job

3. Dad made a <u>fresh</u> pot of coffee this morning.

    newly made   bold   strong

4. We needed to <u>fast</u> a day in order to start our diet the following day.

    be quick   go without food   run

5. Every spring we need to put several bags of <u>lime</u> on our lawn.

    citrus fruit   chemical substance   special soil

6. The bus driver took a <u>left</u> turn in order to arrive on time at school.

    direction   did leave   wrong

7. Did you <u>object</u> when they announced the new rule about not wearing tee-shirts to work?

    a thing   protest   approve

(Turn page)

8. We needed to put the animals in the <u>pen</u> before the storm arrived.

    instrument for writing   enclosed yard   forest

9. Her boss put the sales <u>record</u> on her desk to be copied for the meeting.

    write down   music disk   statement

10. What did you do with the <u>rest</u> of the chocolate cake?

    what is left   sleep   largest piece

11. How do you <u>spell</u> Mississippi?

    period of work   say the letters of a word   write the word

12. They put a new <u>well</u> in our back yard because the old one went dry.

    satisfactory   hole dug for water   stream

38

Name_____ Date_____

Read each group of words below. Underline the pair of words in each group that rhymes. The first one is done for you.

1. <u>eight</u>   lately   <u>wait</u>   waste

2. hopeful   forgetting   setting   fullness

3. clutter   mother   quarter   shutter

4. moan   zone   cloned   climbed

5. shaking   shouting   baking   breaking

6. least   feast   first   finest

7. chilly   sorry   soapy   silly

8. though   taught   bought   boat

9. drizzle   puzzle   nozzle   guzzle

10. snowing   glowing   clowning   crown

11. thigh   hockey   rocket   why

12. rocket   socket   forget   inlet

13. straw   shawl   drawn   draw

14. trash   clash   brush   bench

15. wheat   weed   went   meat

(Turn page)

16.	prune	proof	moon	zoom
17.	theme	robbery	riddle	scream
18.	torn	shown	frown	thorn
19.	brick	stick	stock	stop
20.	rough	thought	tough	thigh

39

Name_____ Date_____

Hinks Pinks

A <u>Hink Pink</u> is made up of two rhyming spelling patterns that make a <u>funny</u> <u>description</u>. Read each definition and see if you can make up a Hink Pink for it. You can work with a partner(s) if you wish. When you are done with this activity sheet, make up your own Hink Pink for Number 20. The first one is done for you.

1. loud bell   _____strong gong_____

2. close/distant automobile   _____

3. impolite man   _____

4. royal jewelry   _____

5. aquatic meal   _____

6. colored beverage   _____

7. ill boy   _____

8. rotund feline   _____

9. uncontrollable youngster   _____

10. touch rodent   _____

11. view insect   _____

12. primate's coat   _____

(Turn page)

13. distant heavenly body _____

14. unpleasant supervisor _____

15. dark bag _____

16. excellent home _____

17. large hog _____

18. naughty father _____

19. water wave _____

20. _____ _____

40

Name_____ **Date**_____

Make up your own <u>Hinks Pinks</u>. A Hink Pink is a rhyming definition of one-syllable words. The first one has been done for you. You may work with a partner(s) if you want, and you may use a dictionary.

1. unhappy father   _____ sad dad _____

2. boat journey   _____

3. Parisian pew   _____

4. kitten doctor   _____

5. eat meal   _____

6. gift evergreen   _____

7. pleasant rodents   _____

8. show money   _____

9. bad instrument   _____

10. loud music   _____

11. rose animal   _____

12. dark fastener   _____

13. water reptile   _____

(Turn page)

14. slippery twig   _____

15. letter container   _____

16. thin boy   _____

17. head ache   _____

18. hog hair   _____

19. evening argument   _____

20. insect container   _____

21. child bed   _____

22. unhappy boy   _____

23. weak bird   _____

24. uncovered seat   _____

25. library burglar   _____

41

Name_____ Date_____

Read this story about a class project. As you read it, mark the double <u>o</u>'s in each word long − or short ˘. If a double <u>o</u> is neither long nor short, do not mark it at all.

Something Worthwhile

Mr. Rankin's fourth-grade class at Martin Luther King School had been brooding for some time, trying to decide on a class project that would be both interesting and worthwhile. After much thought, Shun suggested that the class visit some of the elderly people who lived in a nursing home on his block. He said that some of the elderly people at the home seemed nearly marooned there because some of their relatives were unable to come and visit them often. He also said that some of the residents felt as though they had been uprooted from their own homes when their relatives took them to live in a nursing home.

At the beginning, some of the children were gloomy about the idea of visiting elderly people, and even Mr. Rankin thought the plan might not be successful. However, after some more discussion, the class decided to have Mr. Rankin look into the idea with the director of the nursing home.

After talking to the director, Mr. Rankin told the children in his classroom that they could try out the idea if they wanted to do so. The children decided that each of them would meet once a week with an elderly man or woman whom they would call their "adopted grandparent." Then the children discussed what they would do when they met with their adopted grandparents. Danny suggested that they might bring a good book to read. Latoya thought they could make cookies or candy to give to their adopted grandparents. Tanya suggested that they tell the elderly person about something the class had studied recently in school, such as how Eskimos sometimes live in igloos, how kangaroos can be seen in Australia, or about ships like schooners and sloops. Michael thought that an adopted grandparent might enjoy looking at some cartoons.

(Turn page)

After visiting the nursing home once a week for several months and doing many interesting things with their adopted grandparents, all of the children in Mr. Rankin's classroom at Martin Luther King School decided that they had really enjoyed the experience at the nursing home and had done something worthwhile. However, the elderly people at the nursing home probably benefited the most from this project because it made them feel good and even young again.

42

Name_____ Date_____

Read this story about a child who has some interesting daydreams. The story contains <u>three words</u> with the "aw" sound." As you read each of these words in the story, print the first letter of each word you have underlined <u>in order</u> on the short lines underneath the story. Notice that the vowel is already included in the answer for you. If you correctly locate all of the words, your answer will tell what the child really wanted to do the most.

I Wish I Could

All children daydream about the things they wish they could do. I have daydreams, too. Sometimes I see myself skating on a beautiful pond in the winter. I am twirling around and around, and I never get dizzy. Other times I daydream that I am in a saucer sliding down a snowy hill so fast that I can see the trees whizzing by me. Sometimes I imagine that I am skiing down the side of a mountain streaking in and out of the gates.

At other times I imagine that I am standing at the top of a cliff waiting to dive into the blue ocean below. I listen to the crowd yelling raucously for me to have a great dive. Often I dream that I am surfing in the blue ocean off the Hawaiian Islands. I ride the crest of the waves and never fall off the board. Once in a while I imagine that I am swimming across the English Channel all covered with grease to protect me from the biting cold of the sea.

I have imagined that I am sky diving with a parachute from an airplane. Sometimes I daydream about hang gliding high over a beautiful blue lake on a warm summer day. I am being towed by a big red motorboat, and I see myself rising high into a cloudless sky up over the lake.

Having daydreams is not a fault. I may be able to realize any dream if I try hard enough.

_____ U _____ _____

43

Name_____ **Date**_____

Read this story about a child who has to make a decision about where to go for a special birthday treat. The story contains <u>eleven words</u> with a <u>diphthong</u> (oi, ou, oy, ow). As you read the story, underline each word with a diphthong. When you have finished reading the story, print the first letter of each word you have underlined <u>in order</u> on the short lines below the story. If you correctly locate all of the words containing a diphthong, you will answer this question: Where did the child decide to go for a birthday treat?

Where Should I Go?

I am going to have a birthday next week, and my parents have promised to take me anyplace I want to go. When I heard that they were letting me make the decision myself, I gave a rousing cheer. After all, there are dozens of places in the city that would be super to visit.

Although my dad suggested that we tour an art gallery to see some famous oil paintings, I vetoed that idea because it probably would be boring. I had the thought that it might be thrilling to fish from a charter boat in Lake Michigan, but I decided against that idea. I know I couldn't count on landing any fish.

Although I wanted to please my mother when she suggested that we tour the planetarium, I decided not to kowtow to her wishes in the matter. It is my birthday, after all. Then I suggested that we all go to hear a famous rock group at the stadium in the city. My father and mother agreed to buy tickets for the concert if it pleased me.

Then I thought it might be exciting to watch a rodeo that is coming to the city. I really think that it would be great to see cowboys rope calves and ride Brahma bulls. I really would like to see their outfits, too. I have always been fascinated by ranch life. The thought just occurred to me now that it might be educational to visit a city council meeting, but that might be pretty dull. It would be very enjoyable to visit an amusement park located north of the city. I could go on all of the super rides in the park.

(Turn page)

I suppose that we might attend a big league baseball game, but I'm really not very interested in baseball. Anyway, our teams aren't doing very well this year. We could go to a fancy restaurant and have round steak, but that wouldn't be much of a treat since I like hamburgers better anyway. In a way, I would like to go to the heart of town and see a new movie that stars one of my favorite actors.

I'll have to make my decision soon because I want to have a really special birthday that I'll remember for a long, long time.

—— —— —— ——   —— —— —— —— —— —— ——

44

Name_____ **Date**_____

Read these definitions of <u>vocabulary terms</u>. Complete each word puzzle with the correct letters. You may use a dictionary if you want and work with a partner(s).

1. Give a word for a dangerous condition caused by air bubbles in the blood or tissues that results from a sudden lowering of pressure.

   b ____ ____ ____ ____

2. Give a word for grassy regions in the midwest United States that have few bushes or trees.

   p ____ ____ ____ ____ ____

3. Give a word for the basic unit of living matter or tissue.

   c ____ ____ ____

4. Give a word for an Olympic sport that is played in countries around the world.

   s ____ ____ ____ ____ ____

5. Give a word for a bitter quarrel, perhaps between two families.

   f ____ ____ ____

6. Give a word for something that will float on water and can be used to mark a channel.

   b ____ ____ ____

7. Give a word for an area with steep sides.

   v ____ ____ ____ ____ ____

(Turn page)

8. Give a word that means to ridicule or to tease with scorn.

t ___ ___ ___ ___

9. Give a word for a green stone used in jewelry.

j ___ ___ ___

10. Give a word for a slave in the Middle Ages who worked the land and was sold with the land.

s ___ ___ ___

11. Give a word that means the surrounding or blocking off of a place during a war.

s ___ ___ ___ ___

12. Give a word that means to dwell or to stay in a place.

a ___ ___ ___ ___

13. Give a word that means to run or move with long and easy steps.

l ___ ___ ___

14. Give a word that means to work hard or to labor.

t ___ ___ ___

15. Give a word that means any one of a family of felines.

c ___ ___

45

Name_____ Date_____

Silently read this story about a child in fourth grade. The story contains <u>seven</u> words with the <u>schwa sound</u>. The schwa sound is the sound a vowel (<u>a</u>, <u>e</u>, <u>i</u>, <u>o</u>, or <u>u</u>) makes in the <u>unaccented syllable of a word of two or more syllables</u>. It has about the same sound as short /u/. Although the words <u>a</u> and <u>the</u> are sometimes said to have the schwa sound, **do not** underline them as they contain only one syllable. When you have finished reading the story, print on the short lines below the story the first letter of each word you have underlined <u>in the order</u> you found it in the story. If you correctly find all of the words with the schwa sound, your answer will spell the thing this child likes best about school.

About School

I am in the fourth grade at Juarez School. There are many things I like at school, and some things I don't like very much.

My school is in a rural area. It has a huge playground where all of the students can play. The lady who teaches us is named Mrs. Sanchez. She is very nice, but she can be very strict at times. When she speaks with emphasis, everybody minds. I like to read very much. In fact, I think I read very well. I enjoy animal stories of all kinds. I also like music and art. One of the best things in school is recess, but Mrs. Sanchez disapproves if we play too roughly.

There are some things I don't really like at school. I don't like math very much at all, and I wish I wasn't so ignorant in it. Maybe I wouldn't be if I studied math more in school and at home. I guess it gives me a negative feeling. I don't care for spelling, and I don't do very well on the spelling tests we have in school.

I think I'll be very glad when I am a graduate of Juarez School, but then I guess I'll just have to study more in high school.

____ ____ ____ ____ ____ ____ ____

ANSWER KEYS

1. His dog saw some snakes last night. My brother will try to spear some fish at night. Tim will beat Jack not Dan and Jim when they play ball.

2. My kitten will jump when she can see string. This black snake will kill mice when it can. She smiles when my dog umps.

3. 1. canoe; 2. sentence; 3. penguins; 4. decorate; 5. magician; 6. costume; 7. pioneers; 8. recess; 9. candles; 10. koala; 11. happy; 12. nightmare; 13. violin; 14. zero; 15. perfume

4. 1. prairie; 2. grateful; 3. drowsy; 4. planets; 5. special; 6. dread; 7. platinum; 8. stitch; 9. brooded; 10. scraped

5. 1. fluffy; 2. glider; 3. stern; 4. scornful; 5. privilege; 6. blizzard; 7. brilliant; 8. twilight; 9. spread; 10. spectacular; 11. skim; 12. probably; 13. sleepy

6. 1. gypsy; 2. canary; 3. recite; 4. city; 5. century; 6. gym; 7. bicycle; 8. cyclone; 9. ceiling; 10. census; 11. center; 12. cellar; 13. general; 14. cause; 15. rage; 16. change; 17. gem; 18. ginger; 19. age; 20. nice

7. 1. engine; 2. twice; 3. citizen; 4. cement; 5. voice; 6. comic; 7. cane; 8. circle; 9. comb; 10. accent; 11. cypress; 12. coat; 13. giant; 14. curly; 15. capsule; 16. pencil; 17. decide; 18. danger; 19. energy; 20. percent

8. 1. glacier; 2. blunder; 3. photography; 4. chisel; 5. professions; 6. translated; 7. shutters; 8. shale; 9. thicket; 10. wharf

9. 1. white; 2. shillings; 3. thigh; 4. phantoms; 5. phonics; 6. whippet; 7. thermometer; 8. phase; 9. think; 10. tough

10. 1. competition; 2. ingenious; 3. preposterous; 4. revulsion; 5. impetuous; 6. slight; 7. prematurely; 8. sigh; 9. derrick; 10. positive

11. 1. cohesive; 2. corruption; 3. ominous; 4. excursion; 5. freedom; 6. statement; 7. forward; 8. pottery; 9. different; 10. darkness; 11. right

12. 1. high; 2. bounce; 3. rough; 4. whirlpool; 5. bamboo; 6. skirt; 7. chimpanzee; 8. draft; 9. spectacular; 10. those; 11. hook; 12. volcano; 13. fright; 14. twenty; 15. precious

13. 1. chairs; 2. bosses; 3. gulfs; 4. videos; 5. dishes; 6. benches; 7. beliefs; 8. radios; 9. booklets; 10. tosses; 11. cliffs; 12. waxes; 13. crosses; 14. colleges; 15. trenches; 16. foxes; 17. fishes; 18. matches; 19. taxes; 20. brushes; 21. pencils; 22. lunches; 23. wishes; 24. studios

14. 1. cities; 2. valleys; 3. keys; 4. families; 5. candies; 6. plays; 7. armies; 8. puppies; 9. boys; 10. trolleys; 11. babies; 12. turkeys; 13. caddies; 14. varieties; 15. spies; 16. employs; 17. ladies; 18. flies; 19. cherries; 20. joys. Accept from the students plurals that are correct for words ending in f or fe.

15. 1. gulfs; 2. leaves; 3. cliffs; 4. knives; 5. thieves; 6. beliefs; 7. halves; 8. loaves; 9. chiefs; 10. wives; 11. roofs; 12. lives; 13. wolves; 14. dwarves; 15. scarves; 16. puffs. Accept from the students plurals that are correct for words ending in y.

16. 1. sightless; 2. joyful; 3. penmanship; 4. weekly; 5. childlike; 6. nervousness; 7. thoughtless; 8. failure; 9. warmly; 10. teacher; 11. worthless; 12. loyalty; 13. lengthen; 14. statement; 15. popularize

17. 1. dysfunction; 2. injustice; 3. irregular; 4. underground; 5. hyperactive; 6. onboard; 7. misspell; 8. discontinue; 9. impossible; 10. submarine; 11. semicircle; 12. recycle; 13. uncertain; 14. midnight; 15. illegal

18. 1. comfort; 2. hold; 3. progress; 4. cycle; 5. economic; 6. back; 7. market; 8. ground; 9. script; 10. continue; 11. child; 12. emotion; 13. distant; 14. honest; 15. school; 16. friend; 17. continue; 18. fortunate; 19. social; 20. behave; 21. honor; 22. thought; 23. govern; 24. modern; 25. active; 26. noon; 27. standard; 28. publish; 29. assist; 30. encourage

19. 1. knit; 2. gnat; 3. wrong; 4. wrist; 5. knight; 6. gnaw; 7. knapsack; 8. wrestle; 9. gnu; 10. knot; 11. gnarl; 12. knock; 13. gnash; 14. written; 15. kneecap; 16. wring; 17. kneel; 18. knuckle; 19. gnome; 20. knowledge. Accept correct answers for silent consonant words.

20. 1. ghost; 2. knob; 3. wrong; 4. knife; 5. gnat; 6. wrinkle; 7. kneel; 8. gnome; 9. knuckle; 10. write; 11. wrench; 12. gnarl; 13. ghastly; 14. knack; 15. whip; 16. wrestle; 17. ghetto; 18. wreath; 19. kneecap; 20. knife. Accept correct answers for words with silent letters.

21. 1. crime; 2. sack; 3. four; 4. blow; 5. have; 6. guess; 7. wren; 8. doubt; 9. throw; 10. knit; 11. stitch; 12. plumb; 13. khaki; 14. sigh; 15. there; 16. guard; 17. cuddle; 18. lamb; 19. ghastly; 20. wrong; 21. bright; 22. before; 23. sense; 24. been; 25. though; 26. snore; 27. two; 28. unwrap; 29. subtle; 30. learn; 31. crumb; 32. daughter; 33. racetrack; 34. often; 35. guide; 36. pitch

22. Line 1: grade class extremely; Line 2: weeks seemed day night All; Line 3: class collecting money each neighborhood; Line 4: have disease cripples; Line 5: confines wheelchair; Line 6: class collected ninety dollars thought time; Line 7: treat all efforts; Line 8: suggested class have roller; Line 9: miles Saturday; Line 10: really know; Line 11: were extremely anyway course; Line 12: class near homes some time; Line 13: roller skate all; Line 14: All class right; Line 15: Each roller skates were; Line 16: right size their skates fell; Line 17: tried again Although some well; Line 18: alone funny sight see skate; Line 19: tried grabbing some near walls; Line 20: fell again usually; Line 21: well; Line 22: afternoon; Line 23: Before home each Cokes; Line 24: Somehow taste; Line 25: eaten home time home all; Line 26: class agreed been really; Line 27: day hoped might able roller again; Line 28: someday

23. 1. maid; 2. steel; 3. glue; 4. peach; 5. claim; 6. triad; 7. fruit; 8. cheap; 9. preach; 10. coach; 11. coast; 12. praise; 13. streak; 14. paint; 15. clean; 16. fuel; 17. approach; 18. explain; 19. peanut; 20. cruel.
Accept correct responses to words with long and short vowel combinations.

24. 1. doesn't: does not; 2. aren't: are not; 3. I'll: I will; 4. they'll: they will; 5. couldn't: could not; 6. Didn't: Did not; 7. I'm: I am; 8. Wasn't: Was not; 9. isn't: is not; 10. weren't: were not; 11. you're: you are; 12. I'd: I would, she'd: she would; 13. It's: It is, you'd: you had; 14. doesn't: does not, she'll: she will

25. Top of the page: 1. I'm; 2. she's; 3. we're; 4. he's; 5. it's; 6. they're; 7. didn't; 8. won't; 9. I've; 10. there's. Bottom of the page: 1. could not; 2. cannot; 3. I will; 4. do not; 5. here is; 6. are not; 7. she will; 8. had not; 9. would not; 10. they will

26. 1. bat ter; 2. writ ten; 3. flat ter; 4. Mol ly; 5. rid dle; 6. ap pear; 7. hap pen; 8. fil ler; 9. trol ley; 10. sad dle; 11. er ror; 12. mid dle; 13. op pose; 14. im mense; 15. lit tle; 16. in ning; 17. an nounce; 18. ef fort; 19. plan ning; 20. mis spell. Accept from the students any double consonant responses that are correct.

27. 1. jun/gle 2; 2. my/self 2; 3. un/der 2; 4. to/day 2; 5. card 1; 6. with/out 2; 7. ex/plain 2; 8. strong 1; 9. fi/gure 2; 10. lan/guage 2; 11. dis/tance 2; 12. re/gion 2; 13. moun/tain 2; 14. in/for/mal 3; 15. sub/ma/rine 3; 16. mis/for/tune 3; 17. un/do/ing 3; 18. in/form/ant 3; 19. ir/re/spon/sive 4; 20. dis/tress/ful 3

28. 1. ex/er/cise 3; 2. com/mon 2; 3. pat/tern 2; 4. dif/fer/ent 3; 5. in/ter/est 3; 6. cer/tain 2; 7. ta/ble 2; 8. o/mit 2; 9. re/cord 2; 10. vil/lage 2; 11. is/land 2; 12. ca/pa/ble 3; 13. re/mem/ber 3; 14. syl/la/ble 3; 15. in/cre/di/ble 4; 16. dis/cov/er 3; 17. sud/den/ly 3; 18. ma/ter/nal 3; 19. quick/ly 2; 20. un/like/ly 3; 21. si/tu/a/tion 4; 22. re/pre/sent 3; 23. how/ev/er 3. Accept students' responses that are correct. Syllable challenge: Accept correct responses.

29. 1. l; 2. l; 3. s; 4. l; 5. s; 6. l; 7. l; 8. l; 9. l; 10. l; 11. l; 12. s; 13. l; 14. s; 15. l; 16. s; 17. l; 18. l; 19. s; 20. s; 21. s; 22. l; 23. l; 24. s; 25. l; 26. s; 27. l; 28. l; 29. s; 30. l. Accept correct responses for ee and ea words.

30. 1. $\bar{e}$; 2. $\bar{\imath}$; 3. y; 4. $\bar{e}$; 5. $\bar{\imath}$; 6. y; 7. $\bar{\imath}$; 8. y; 9. $\bar{e}$; 10. y; 11. $\bar{e}$; 12. $\bar{e}$; 13. $\bar{\imath}$; 14. $\bar{e}$; 15. y; 16. $\bar{\imath}$; 17. $\bar{e}$; 18. $\bar{e}$; 19. $\bar{\imath}$; 20. $\bar{\imath}$; 21. $\bar{\imath}$; 22. y; 23. $\bar{\imath}$; 24. $\bar{e}$

31. 1. keep-hold, story-tale, income-earnings, end-finish, hurry-rush; 2. junk-waste, strength-power, frequent-often, bother-annoy, close-shut; 3. work-labor, still-silent, take-grab, mistake-blunder, pain-ache; 4. vast-huge, try-attempt, find-locate, value-worth, new-fresh

32. 1. above-below, easy-hard, crooked-straight, fiction-fact, empty-full; 2. tall-short, teacher-student, north-south, rapid-slow, weep-laugh; 3. wet-dry, top-bottom, now-then, sour-sweet, remember-forget; 4. hurry-slow, often-seldom, melt-freeze, stranger-friend, wild-tame

33. 1. totals; 2. taller; 3. started; 4. sadness; 5. strolled; 6. sheets; 7. hating; 8. forbids; 9. rushing; 10. knowing; 11. happily; 12. created; 13. slowed; 14. hazardous/perilous; 15. thieves/crooks. Accept from the students any antonyms and synonyms that make sense.

34. 1. birthday; 2. grandmother, oatmeal; 3. outlaw, mailman's; 4. Somewhere, hairbrush; 5. popcorn, raincoat; 6. railroad, policeman; 7. rainbow, southwest, sunshine; 8. blueberry, Rosemarie's, raincoat; 9. peanuts, cupcakes; 10. shipmate, shipwreck, sometime, lifeboat; 11. highlight, newspaper, drugstores; 12. dragonfly, doghouse, football, outside; 13. steamboat, weekend, storyteller's; 14. homesick, inside, bedroom; 15. birthday, everyone, earache

35. 1. ate, steak; 2. write, who's; 3. Some, do; 4. sell, new; 5. forward, flower; 6. know, there; 7. pale, pair; 8. our, deer; 9. steal, would; 10. polls, you; 11. beat, dessert; 12. stairs, higher, wood; 13. weak, bear; 14. sale, karat; 15. whether, piece, bowl

36. Who's/whose: 1. Whose; 2. who's; 3. Who's; 4. Whose; 5. whose; 6. who's
You're/your: 1. your; 2. You're; 3. you're; 4. you're; 5. your; 6. your

37. 1. condition; 2. group of musicians; 3. newly made; 4. go without food; 5. chemical substance; 6. direction; 7. protest; 8. enclosed yard; 9. statement; 10. what is left; 11. say the letters of a word; 12. hole dug for water

38. 1. eight, wait; 2. forgetting, setting; 3. clutter, shutter; 4. moan, zone; 5. shaking, baking; 6. least, feast; 7. chilly, silly; 8. taught, bought; 9. puzzle, guzzle; 10. snowing, glowing; 11. thigh, why; 12. rocket, socket; 13. straw, draw; 14. trash, clash; 15. wheat, meat; 16. prune, moon; 17. theme, scream; 18. torn, thorn; 19. brick, stick; 20. rough, tough

39. 1. strong gong; 2. far car; 3. rude dude; 4. king ring; 5. fish dish; 6. pink drink; 7. sick Dick; 8. fat cat; 9. wild child; 10. pat rat; 11. see bee; 12. ape cape; 13. far star; 14. cross boss; 15. black sack; 16. best nest; 17. big pig; 18. bad Dad; 19. lake wake; 20. Accept any Hink Pink answer that makes sense and rhymes.

40. 1. sad Dad; 2. ship trip; 3. French bench; 4. pet vet; 5. munch lunch (brunch); 6. free tree; 7. nice mice; 8. flash cash; 9. bum drum; 10. strong song; 11. pink mink; 12. black tack; 13. lake snake; 14. slick stick; 15. mail pail; 16. slim Jim (Tim, Kim) or frail male; 17. brain pain; 18. pig wig; 19. night fight; 20. bug jug (mug); 21. tot cot; 22. sad lad; 23. frail quail; 24. bare chair; 25. book crook

41.

School	look	school	looking
brooding	classroom	igloos	cartoons
marooned	good	kangaroos	room
uprooted	book	schooners	School
gloomy	cookies	sloops	good

42. saucer, raucously, fault: s u r f

43. rousing, oil, count, kowtow, cowboys, outfits, now, council, enjoyable, round, town: r o c k c o n c e r t

44. 1. bends; 2. prairie; 3. cell; 4. soccer; 5. feud; 6. buoy; 7. valley; 8. taunt; 9. jade; 10. serf; 11. siege; 12. abide; 13. lope; 14. toil; 15. cat

45. rural, emphasis, animal, disapproves, ignorant, negative, graduate: r e a d i n g